# Celebrate Life, Food and Wine

Varun Inamdar



OM
Om Books International

Published in 2015

Om Books International

Corporate and Editorial Office
A-12, Sector 64, Noida - 201301, Uttar Pradesh, India
Phone: +91-120 4774100
Email: editorial@ombooks.com
Website: www.ombooksinternational.com

Sales Office
107, Daryaganj, New Delhi - 110 002, India
Phone: +91 11 4000 9000, 2326 3363, 2326 5303
Fax: +91 11 2327 8091
Email: sales@ombooks.com
Website: www.ombooks.com

Content Research and Editing: Vinita Bhatia
Food Photography: Piyush Singh, Gauri Karnik and Hardika Thakkar
Food Styling: Varun Inamdar
Studio Kitchen: Food-E:Culinary Experts
Food Team: Chef Aditi Goel, Gagandeep Singh Narula and Pankaj Dalvi
Design and layout: Shraboni Roy



ISBN: 978-93-85031-24-3

Printed in India

10 9 8 7 6 5 4 3 2 1

# FOREWORD

My family has an age-old tradition. Every time, we have any reason to celebrate, out comes a bottle of wine (sometimes more than one) and we drink to good health and fortune. This got me thinking on how wine has always been a quintessential part of celebrations for most households, and how even more families are making this ritual a part of their lifestyle.

It gives me great pleasure to introduce this book, which is our effort to make it easy not just to cook celebratory dishes with wine, but also to pair them with the right varietal. After all, there is a perfect wine for every occasion, for every cuisine and for every budget.

Chef Varun Inamdar has done a fantastic job of presenting some of the classic Indian dishes in an entirely new light. I am confident you will never again think of a biryani or roast chicken without recalling the recipes from this book.

Vinita Bhatia's research on how wine and celebrations go hand-in-hand will solve the frequent dilemma customers have when it comes to selecting the perfect varietal for any occasion. Be it a casual brunch, a family lunch or entertaining friends for dinner, a quick peek at the pairing profiles will give you all the information you need about rejoicing with wines.

I would also like to thank Om Books International for their contribution in making this an easy-to-navigate book.

Finally, here's raising a toast to all the good times in your life, which we hope you enjoy with a glass of good wine.

*—Adrian Pinto*

# History of Wine

## "In wine, there is truth."

—Pliny the Elder, Roman philosopher

Anyone who has visited the Egyptian pyramids is unlikely to have missed the wall murals showing pharaohs drinking wine or the images of their slaves making wine. It is a well known fact that when pharaohs were entombed with their slaves, concubines and wealth after their death, their favourite wine bottles were also buried with them, so that they could enjoy themselves in the afterlife.

This fact led some researchers to deduce that wine making and drinking probably has its origin in Egypt around 3000 BC. However, that is the beauty of this drink, which was often called the elixir of the gods. It is hard to determine which region was the exact origin of grape cultivation for wine making.

A few years ago, archaeologists stumbled upon what could possibly be termed the world's oldest known winery in an Armenian cave, which they pegged to be at least 6,000 years old. Similar archaeological finds in China, Greece, Rome and parts of the Middle East have unearthed wine bottles, making their task of determining the origin of winemaking more difficult and contentious.

### Wine Finds Favour Globally

In ancient Greece, wine was offered to gods to invoke their blessings. The Greek historian Thucydides even remarked that it was only the cultivation of wine and olives that helped people in the region to mould their barbaric ways to a more evolved civilization. However, the Romans gave wine its cult status, where a glass of wine with every meal soon became part of their lifestyle. This is evident from the fact that many small cafés sprung throughout the empire where this beverage was stocked and sold. The demand for wine became so popular that vast tracts of land in Rome were devoted for cultivation of grapes.

What is also interesting is that as Christianity gained preeminence throughout Europe, winemaking received a fillip, given its use during Mass. Monks started producing wine for this purpose and their own consumption. Soon merchants in the region realised that there was a market for these full-bodied wines that were mixed with various spices and condiments, and started exporting them to the further corners of the world.

As trade routes became more established, European wines made their way into Asia Minor and Central Asia. Though countries like China were already producing wine from grapes back then, the local produce was nudged aside by rice and other grain-based wine. Around 220 AD, monarchs of the Han dynasty started importing grape seeds from the Middle East to produce sweeter tasting wine, which they believed did not leave an acidic taste on the palate or heaviness in the head, if imbibed too much.

Soon, winemakers started developing distinctive strains of grapes to make wine that had unique flavours, colours and characteristics. Today, wine has become the ideal everyday drink compatible with any meal or any occasion. It is not just something to sip on, but has become a drink to savour and luxuriate in.

# Cooking with Wine

## "I cook with wine. Sometimes I even add it to the food."
—WC Fields, American actor and writer

The rising interest about wine might make one believe that cooking with wine is a new trend. On the contrary, wine has been an important medium of cooking for centuries now. The earliest records of this technique can be attributed to Romans who used a concentrate of unfermented grape juice to lend colour to food and sometimes sweeten it. People in the Mediterranean region, too, used full-bodied wine to season their meat dishes, often skipping other condiments.

Wine lends a rich flavour to any dish, irrespective of what you are preparing. Of course, you need to remember one rule of thumb while cooking with wine – avoid cheap varieties and stick to those that you would sip on gladly. You also have to be very careful not to overcook wine as it could end up giving a bitter taste to the final dish.

Here are some of the more common ways in which you can cook with wine:

**Reduction:** This process calls for simmering wine on low heat until it thickens slightly to a thick sauce like consistency. This is perfect when you have a half-full bottle of wine that you do not want to cork and store away. Reduction intensifies the wine's flavour and you can either drizzle it on dishes, such as meat fillets, or glaze ingredients, similar to what we did with 'Honey Glazed Carrots' (page 20-21).

**Marinade:** Wine makes for a great marinade because its acidity can permeate through meat well. When mixed with other ingredients, it gives the meat an exquisite zest. The 'Festive Mutton Biryani' (page 40-41) uses this technique and you can try it out to see how the inclusion of wine makes all the difference to this classic dish.

**Poaching:** The French figured out a long time ago that steeping fruits in wine turns it into a classic dessert. Immersing fruits in wine and poaching it helps retain the intense flavour of the fruit and the wine respectively, complementing the flavour of each without overwhelming the other. Curious to try this out? Check out the easy to prepare 'Mulled Wine' (page 14-15).

**Infusion:** You can create magic by infusing wine with various ingredients like fruits, berries, spices or condiments. All you need is some imagination and good wine. The longer you infuse ingredients in wine, the more complex the flavour of the finished product. So, get your culinary creativity flowing by following the example of 'Festive Soup With Halwa' (page 54-55), and you will know what we mean.

These are just few of the many techniques where wine can be employed for cooking. It is heartening to see celebrated chefs globally experiment with new ways to include wine in the preparation of food. This has sparked further interest amongst home cooks who cannot wait to revisit traditional recipes and represent it in a unique fashion during festivities and celebrations.

# Introducing Nine Hills Wines

## "Wine is bottled poetry."

—Robert Louis Stevenson, British poet and author

There is a quaint story about how the 'Nine Hills' name came about. This wine brand from Pernod Ricard India gets its name from the nine hills surrounding Nashik.

Every drop of the Nine Hills brand is under constant care of French master winemaker, Jean Manuel Jacquinot, who has fused old world traditions with innovative viticulture and winemaking practices to yield powerful, yet balanced, wines with classic aromas, rich texture and lingering flavours.

So whether you prefer the zesty whites or suave reds, Nine Hills winery caters to your every need. Their vineyard currently grows five varietals – Chenin Blanc, Sauvignon Blanc, Cabernet Sauvignon, Viognier and Shiraz.

The first thing that strikes you about the Nine Hills Chenin Blanc is its golden hue. This medium dry wine has a crisp and refreshing flavour, with mildly floral aromas and a hint of honey. The fruity notes are more pronounced and leave you in no doubt that this is a wine that can hold its own when paired with rich and classic food.

The light-bodied Nine Hills Sauvignon Blanc has a rounded structure with a clean finish. This crisp and dry wine, with its nuanced flavours of passion fruit, pineapple, gooseberry and fresh lime can highlight subtle flavours in food.

The attractive deep red colour of the Nine Hills Cabernet Sauvignon gives an indication of its elegance. A dry, medium-bodied wine with well balanced acidity, its soft tannins tantalise the taste buds, while its lingering finish holds on to its cherry, vanilla and capsicum aromas.

The aroma-rich Nine Hills Viognier exudes a complex bouquet of peach, lychees and violets. Its pale gold colour comes shining through when served chilled with some snacks or lightly cooked seafood or meat.

When you open a bottle of the Nine Hills Shiraz, be prepared for a distinct smoky aroma along with a basket of fruity flavours of cherries and strawberries. The mild acidity of this full-bodied wine has soft velvety tannins, which is a perfect accompaniment for most Indian treats.

Apart from the deep red Cabernet Sauvignon and Shiraz wines, Nine Hills also makes the finest 'Reserve', from these two varietals, which are slightly shrivelled in the golden sunshine of the slopes. And Shiraz, of course, also has an elegant Rosé varietal with a clean, crisp finish.

# Celebrating With Nine Hills Wines

## "Let us celebrate the occasion with wine and sweet words."

—Plautus, Roman philosopher

Wine has been an inseparable part of festivities for ages. The ancient Greeks even held an annual festival of wine, called 'Anthestiria', to honour their god, Dionysus.

Over the years, clinking glasses of wine has become symbolic with celebrations and festivities. What has also helped establish wine as a celebratory beverage is the fact that it can be paired with a wide array of foods. Be it the casual pizza or the classic roast chicken, wine is versatile enough to go with any dish you can conceive. And it especially pairs well with food that is traditionally prepared during most Indian festivals.

Take the case of the crunchy mathri, a staple savoury prepared during most Indian celebrations. Often had as is, adventurous home cooks have tried using it as a snack, but very rarely as a base for a variety of toppings, just like we have with the 'Pumpkin On Mathris' (page 18-19). Serve this snack with the medium-bodied Nine Hills Cabernet Sauvignon since its hints of cherry, vanilla and capsicum will heighten the flavour of the spices used in the mathri, as does any drink containing alcohol.

The quintessential 'Pan Roasted Potatoes' (page 22-23) makes for a suitable accompaniment to any meal, festive or otherwise. Pair it with the Nine Hills Reserve Cabernet Sauvignon and watch how the suggestion of mild spices in the wine with its bouquet of vanilla transforms this humble dish into a culinary masterpiece.

No festival meal in India is complete without a rice preparation. Contrast the creamy 'Red Rice Risotto' (page 30-31) with the light-bodied Nine Hills Sauvignon Blanc, which has a crisp finish and refreshing fruity flavour. You will find the complex flavours of the risotto meld perfectly with the intense notes of passion fruit, pineapple, gooseberry and fresh lime of the wine.

Now, the voluptuous 'Prawn Moilee' (page 38-39) can command its spot in the limelight. The mildly sweet Nine Hills Viognier with its delicate fruity flavours plays the perfect supporting role to this creamy dish, without taking away from the aroma of the seafood.

Pairing wine with food has come a long way from the time when people would blatantly suggest white wine with white meat and red wine with red meat. Today, consumers take the pains to learn as much as they can about the tasting notes and flavours of a particular wine before intelligently pairing it with food. We have taken the guessing out of the game for you, by suggesting wines that go fabulously with the recipes in this book based on our experiences in the kitchen and vineyards.

# Wine Pairing Notes

## "Wine and cheese are ageless companions, like June and moon or good people and noble ventures."

—Mary Frances Kennedy Fisher, American food writer

At first glance, trying to understand how wine should be paired with certain types of food, based on its notes and flavours, can be quite intimidating. But it need not be so, because there is no such rule as the perfect wine-food pairing!

Once you get over this mental hurdle, you can pair any food with any type of wine as long as each complements or accentuates the flavour of the other. It is all about striking the right balance. However, if there ever was a rulebook about wine and food pairing, it would surely include some of the following pointers:

**Enhance, not influence:** Choose wines that will accentuate, or at least will not overwhelm, the flavour of a particular dish.

**Pay attention to looks:** It stands to reason that a light-coloured wine will go best with light-coloured food. So, a salad with mild dressing is paired best with a crisp Chenin Blanc or Sauvignon Blanc. For food that has dense hues, like gravies or red meat, opt for wines with darker shades like a full-bodied Shiraz or a Cabernet Sauvignon.

**Age matters:** While picking up a bottle of wine, check its vintage. Older wines have more subtle flavours. So serve it with dishes that will not overpower their subtlety.

The bottom line to wine pairing is that there are no rules; especially in current times when traditional dishes are getting a makeover with contemporary techniques and ingredients. Do not be afraid to experiment – for all you know, you might come up with an unusual wine pairing that is a winner all the way. If still in doubt, the adjoining ready reckoner will help you decide on what wine to choose for a particular dish.

# Wine Pairing Ready Reckoner

| Wine Name | Grape Varietal | Colour | Characteristics | Notes/ Aromas | Food Pairing |
|---|---|---|---|---|---|
| **Nine Hills Shiraz** | Shiraz | Deep red with violet hues | Full-bodied with soft velvety tannins | Fruity notes of strawberries and cherries | Spicy grilled meats, egg-based curries, parathas and mildly spiced cuisines of Bengal, Bihar and Central India. |
| Nine Hills Shiraz Rosé | Shiraz | Shiny pink with violet hues | Light and crisp with fruity aromas and a refreshing clean finish | Light notes of berries, rose blossoms and black cherries | Salads and appetizers. Also pairs perfectly well with white-rinded cheese, mushrcoms, spiced tea cakes, muffins and fruit tarts. |
| **Nine Hills Shiraz Reserve** | Shiraz | Deep purple | Full-bodied with well balanced acidity and soft tannins | Fresh fruits, nuts, coffee, vanilla | Barbecue, cheese, egg-based curries and light vegetarian meals. |
| Nine Hills Cabernet Sauvignon | Cabernet Sauvignon | Terracotta red with purple highlights | Well balanced acidity with soft tannins | Mild notes of cherries, vanilla and capsicums | Hard cheeses, blue cheese, braised meats, stews, all kinds of lentil-based dishes, pizzas, dark chocclate and heavily spiced foods from Karnataka, Eastern India, Maharashtra and Kerala. |
| **Nine Hills Cabernet Sauvignon Reserve** | Cabernet Sauvignon | Deep terracotta red | Well balanced acidity with soft velvety tannins and a lingering finish | Cherries, light spices, black berries and vanillas | Cheese, lightly spiced Punjabi tandoori meats and vegetarian dishes. |
| Nine Hills Sauvignon Blanc | Sauvignon Blanc | Pale golden | Crisp with balanced acidity | Notes of passion fruits, pineapples and fresh limes | Salads, seafood, tomato-based curries, savouries, poppadums, fried fish, tandoori fish, Kashmiri morels, etc. |
| **Nine Hills Chenin Blanc** | Chenin Blanc | Golden | Light floral with slight musky flavour | Honey and fruits | Accompaniments like kachumber, koshimbir or savories like chaat and crunchy snacks. It also pairs well with Gujarati dishes. |
| Nine Hills Viognier | Viognier | Pale yellow | Crisp, refreshing and light on the palate | Fruity notes of peaches and lychees with elegant floral notes | Salads, seafood and creamy stews. It also pairs well with sharp tasting vegetables like aubergine and bitter gourd, or those with bland overtones like cauliflower. |

# CONTENTS

# Mulled Wine

*This Cabernet Sauvignon-based cocktail, spiced with a posy of herbs and spices, is a perfect conversation starter during an evening celebration with family and friends.*

## Ingredients

750 ml Cabernet Sauvignon
60 gm sugar
1-inch cinnamon
A sprig of rosemary
3 unpeeled oranges, cut into roundels
2 unpeeled red apples, cut into thick juliennes
Few mint leaves, for garnish
4 orange slices, for garnish

## Method

1. Place a saucepan on medium flame and pour the wine into it.
2. Add the sugar, cinnamon and rosemary. Let this mixture simmer and keep stirring until the sugar has dissolved.
3. Lower the flame. Add the orange roundels and let it poach in this simmering wine for 15-20 minutes.
4. Remove the poached orange pieces. Cut the roundels into half and keep aside.
5. Drop the half orange pieces into the Rolly Polly serving glass. Place apple juliennes in each glass and strain wine into it.
6. Serve warm.

**Quick tip: Bundle the herbs and condiments in a muslin cloth before cooking them in the pan. This makes it easier to remove them at one go.**

Pairing: Cabernet Sauvignon with natural notes of cherry, vanilla and capsicum is ideal for this drink.

Serves: 4
Time required: 25 minutes
Ease of preparation: Easy
Flavour profile: NA

# Pepper Pinch

*This golden hued Viognier and peach cordial cocktail is a sight to behold. Its sweetness is perfectly balanced by the subtle warmth of green chillies and sprinkles of Himalayan pink salt.*

## Ingredients

2 green chillies

750 ml Viognier, chilled

150 ml peach schnapps

A few dashes of Angostura bitters

½ tsp Himalayan pink salt

4 green chillies, slit partially, for garnish

## Method

1. Chill a snifter glass.
2. Muddle 2 green chillies to unlock their flavour and intensity.
3. Stir all ingredients, except salt and the muddled green chilly, in a large pitcher.
4. Strain the mixture and pour into glasses.
5. Balance the slit green chilly on the edge of the glass for garnish.
6. Serve chilled.

**Quick tip: The colder your wine, the lesser ice you will have to use, which means lesser dilution of the wine.**

Pairing: Made with Viognier for its natural floral notes and peach-like aroma.

Serves: 4
Time required: 15 minutes
Ease of preparation: Easy
Flavour profile: 

# Pumpkin On Mathris

*When an Italian bruschetta meets an Indian Mathri, it is a match made in heaven. Especially when it has a generous smear of onion jam, topped with sautéed pumpkin and cottage cheese crumble.*

## Ingredients

16 readymade Mathris (flat deep-fried flour biscuits)

**For red onion jam**

2 tbsp olive oil

200 gm red onions, sliced fine

30 gm sugar

Sprig of fresh thyme leaves

Salt, to taste

100 ml Cabernet Sauvignon

**For pumpkin**

2 tbsp olive oil

300 gm pumpkin, peeled, deseeded and diced into 1-cm squares

Salt, to taste

**For garnishing**

50 gm cottage cheese, crumbled

1 tsp black pepper, freshly crushed

Fresh mint leaves

## Method

**For red onion jam**

1. Heat olive oil in a pan.
2. Sauté the onions for a couple of minutes till it starts changing colour.
3. Add sugar, thyme leaves, salt and the wine.
4. Reduce the flame and cook till the onions are soft and well cooked.
5. When the onions are soft and sticky, turn off the heat. Keep aside.

**For pumpkin**

1. Heat oil in a pan.
2. Stir fry the pumpkin in olive oil and salt till cooked yet holding a firm shape. Keep aside.

**For assembling**

1. Place the Mathris on a serving plate.
2. Smear a teaspoonful of warm onion jam on it.
3. Top with pumpkin pieces.
4. Sprinkle cottage cheese, black pepper and mint leaves. Serve warm.

**Quick tip: Slow cooking is the secret behind delicious onion jam. Cook it on low flame stirring at regular intervals to avoid burning.**

Pairing: Made using, and goes perfectly well, with Cabernet Sauvignon for its natural capsicum like notes. The wine's full bodied nature adds to the beauty of the jam.

Serves: 4
Time required: 1 hour
Ease of preparation: Medium
Flavour profile:

# Honey Glazed Carrots

*This classical French dish features tender carrot sticks in a honey-laced buttery glaze, nuanced with star anise and fresh dill leaves. The sprinkling of crumbled tofu adds to its creaminess.*

## Ingredients

50 gm salted butter

600 gm baby carrots, cut half lengthwise

2 star anise

½ tsp salt

15 ml honey

80 ml Chenin Blanc

¼ tsp white pepper

**For garnishing**

Few dill sprigs

40 gm tofu, crumbled

## Method

1. Melt the butter in a pan over medium-high heat.
2. Add the carrots. Stir in star anise and toss to combine.
3. Sprinkle salt over carrots and sauté for 3-4 minutes.
4. Add the honey and toss to combine.
5. Add the wine to deglaze the pan.
6. Cover the pan. Reduce the heat and cook for another 3 minutes.
7. Uncover the pan and increase heat. Toss the carrots once or twice to keep them moving, and cook away most of the liquid.
8. Turn off the heat and serve the carrots hot, garnished with some dill leaves and tofu.

**Quick tip: This dish can be prepared and glazed in advance and later served warm. This way you can relax with your guests and not toil away in the kitchen.**

Pairing: You can serve this dish with the same varietal you cooked it in, since the Chenin Blanc's subtle fruity notes complements the dish.

Serves: 4
Time required: 30 minutes
Ease of preparation: Easy
Flavour profile:

# Pan Roasted Potatoes

*This festive dish is conventionally roasted in an oven. But the pan roasting technique gives the potatoes a delicious makeover. The splashes of Cabernet Sauvignon Reserve, with some thyme and black pepper in the marinade, breathe new life into these spuds.*

## Ingredients

800 gm baby potatoes
5-6 garlic cloves
1 tbsp black pepper, freshly ground
250 ml Cabernet Sauvignon Reserve
Few sprigs of fresh thyme
4 tbsp refined oil
Salt, to taste

## Method

1. Wash and lightly scrape the baby potatoes, but don't remove the skin entirely. Cut a few in half at random.
2. In a separate bowl, mix all the other ingredients together to form an emulsion.
3. Pour this marinade over the potatoes and allow them to steep for at least ½ hour.
4. Place a broad cooking pan on high flame.
5. Add the potatoes and stir till 75% of the liquid evaporates.
6. Cover the pan with a lid and lower the flame.
7. Allow the potatoes to cook till they are done, but check repeatedly to prevent them from getting burnt.
8. Uncover the pan and increase heat.
9. Toss the potatoes once or twice till remaining wine evaporates.
10. Turn off the heat and serve hot.

**Quick tip: Prick the potatoes with a toothpick or fork. This allows the spuds to better absorb the marinade while steeping. You can also marinate the potatoes overnight to help the juices permeate it totally.**

Pairing: Best cooked and paired with Cabernet Sauvignon Reserve for its fragrant aromas of light spices, which add an underlying flavour during pan roasting.

Serves: 4
Time required: 1 hour
Ease of preparation: Easy
Flavour profile: 

# Masala Poppadum

*A celebratory meal is incomplete without nibbling on some crunchy masala poppadums. Here is an interesting reinterpretation of this classic snack.*

## Ingredients

150 ml Cabernet Sauvignon
5-6 red millet poppadums
2 tbsp unsalted butter, melted
2 red onions, finely chopped
5-6 cherry tomatoes, quartered
1 tbsp fresh parsley leaves, finely chopped
1 tsp chilly powder
Salt, to taste

## Method

1. Pour wine in a deep bottomed pan and let it simmer till it is reduced to 2 tablespoon.
2. Using a tong, roast poppadums over flame, ensuring they do not get burnt.
3. Brush some melted butter over roasted poppadums.
4. Arrange these on a plate. Top with onions, tomatoes and parsley.
5. Sprinkle chilly powder and salt.
6. Drizzle some warm red wine reduction. Serve warm.

**Quick tip: This dish tastes great with deep fried poppadums. However, if you are health conscious, microwave poppadums thrice for 5 seconds each time and omit butter from the recipe.**

Pairing: Cabernet Sauvignon with natural notes of cherry, vanilla and capsicum adds an element of sweet surprise to the crisp bite. It also balances the chilly sprinkled on the poppadums.

Serves: 4
Time required: 15 minutes
Ease of preparation: Easy
Flavour profile:

# Barbeque Shrimps

*An eternal classic, this is amongst the easiest nibbles you can put on a celebratory table. The natural sweetness of the shrimps is perfectly balanced with chilly, garlic and lemon juice.*

## Ingredients

18-20 large shrimps with tail, shelled and deveined

**For barbeque sauce**

2 tbsp refined oil

2 onions, sliced

1 tbsp garlic, minced

100 ml Sauvignon Blanc

2 tbsp tomato ketchup

2 tsp chilly flakes

1 tbsp castor sugar

Salt, to taste

**For salad**

1 onion, sliced

1 tomato, sliced

Microgreens, as preferred

Salt, to taste

## Method

**For the barbeque sauce**

1. Heat a thick bottomed iron pan.
2. Add oil and sauté onions and garlic till onions turn translucent.
3. Deglaze the pan with white wine.
4. Add ketchup, chilly flakes, sugar and salt. Reduce this syrup till it turns thick and is half the quantity.
5. Add lemon juice and stir well.
6. Marinate shrimps in this warm barbeque sauce for ½ hour.
7. Preheat oven to 200°C.
8. Place shrimps on a baking tray and bake in preheated oven for 12 minutes.
9. In a salad bowl, toss onions, tomatoes, microgreens and salt.
10. Serve alongside the warm prawns.

**Quick tip: To extract juice out of a lemon, microwave an entire lemon for 5 seconds and then squeeze the same for maximum yield.**

Pairing: Sauvignon Blanc with its crisp lemon and passion fruit aroma goes perfectly with this appetizer.

Serves: 4
Time required: 1 hour
Ease of preparation: Easy
Flavour profile:

# Vegetable Khurchan Quesadillas

*This classic Mexican dish gets a healthy makeover with whole wheat quesadillas encasing vegetables seared in the Shiraz Reserve. A light sprinkling of low fat milk cheese adds to the nutrition content and makes it full of life.*

## Ingredients

**For the quesadillas**

450 gm whole wheat flour
1 tsp salt
225 ml chilled water
1 tbsp refined oil

**For the filling**

2 tbsp garlic oil
150 gm baby corns, sliced
150 gm mushrooms, quartered
150 gm zucchini, sliced into roundels
150 gm assorted bell peppers, thickly sliced
100 ml Shiraz Reserve
Salt, to taste
1 tsp fresh oregano
1 tsp freshly ground pepper

**For assembling**

150 gm feta cheese

## Method

1. Sift whole wheat flour and salt in a bowl. Mix with oil and water and knead to form a semi-soft dough.
2. Cover with damp muslin cloth and let the dough rest for 30 minutes.
3. After ½ hour, knead the dough again. Make lemon-sized balls and roll them into thin 8-inch discs.
4. Roast both sides on a hot griddle, till done.

**For the filling**

1. Heat garlic oil in a pan.
2. Add sliced vegetables and sear on high flame till it is lightly charred.
3. Add wine, salt, pepper and oregano and cook till absorbed by the vegetables. Keep aside.

**For assembling**

1. Spoon the vegetables on one half of the bread.
2. Sprinkle some feta cheese and fold the other half of bread. Serve warm.

**Quick tip: For homemade garlic oil, mash 6-7 garlic cloves with the skin on and fry them in 100 ml oil till lightly brown. Strain the browned garlic and retain oil for further use.**

Pairing: Shiraz Reserve for its full-bodied, soft velvety tannins and well balanced acidity.

Serves: 4
Time required: 1 hour
Ease of preparation: Medium
Flavour profile: 

# Red Rice Risotto

*Our take on the classic Risotto Printanière is packed with flavour, courtesy the bouquet of various vegetables and the starch released by unpolished red rice. The Sauvignon Blanc lends some extra impact to make it a stellar dish.*

## Ingredients

200 gm unpolished red rice
15 ml olive oil
25 gm onions, minced
100 gm carrots, diced
50 gm peas, shelled
50 gm cauliflower, cut into florets
75 ml Sauvignon Blanc
750 ml vegetable stock
Salt, to taste
25 gm salted butter
25 gm Parmesan cheese, grated

Serves: 4
Time required: 1 hour
Ease of preparation: Medium
Flavour profile: NA

Pairing: Sauvignon Blanc with its deep fruity aromas and subtle notes of fresh lime adds to the intensity of the unpolished red rice.

## Method

1. Wash the red rice in running water and soak it for ½ hour.
2. In a pan, heat olive oil. Sauté onions till translucent.
3. Add the rice and continue stirring until the edges of rice turn translucent while the center is opaque.
4. Once the aroma of toasted rice fills the kitchen, add the vegetables. Stir for a few seconds to coat them in oil.
5. Deglaze the pan with wine.
6. Boil the vegetable stock in another pan. Add the boiling stock, ladle by ladle, to the rice and and continue stirring.
7. Add salt to taste. Once the liquid is almost absorbed, add another ladle of the stock. Continue this till all the stock is evaporated, while stirring continuously.
8. Add the butter and parmesan cheese. Give a quick stir, cover the pan and rest for 2 minutes.
9. Serve hot.

**Quick tip: To make vegetable stock quickly, dip the trimmings of all vegetables in cold water. Boil the same water for 5 minutes and simmer for 15 minutes on low flame. Strain and reserve for further use.**

# Tawa Naan Pizza

*Make a pizza base with naan on a griddle with some wine-based tomato sauce, pan-fried fig slices and goat cheese. Easy, isn't it?*

## Ingredients

**For the naan pizza base**

400 gm refined flour
1 tsp salt
30 ml refined oil
180 ml water

**For the pizza sauce**

2 tbsp olive oil
2-3 garlic cloves
100 ml Cabernet Sauvignon Reserve
500 gm ripe tomatoes, grated
4-5 basil leaves
Salt, to taste

**For the topping**

100 gm fresh corn
300 ml Cabernet Sauvignon Reserve
4-5 ripe figs, sliced

**For assembling**

75 gm feta cheese
Few sprigs of coriander
Salt, to taste

Pairing: The velvety tannins and light spicy aroma of Cabernet Sauvignon Reserve go perfectly with a crisp pizza.

## Method

**For the naan dough**

1. In a bowl, sift flour with salt. Add oil and water and knead to form a soft dough.
2. Cover it with a damp muslin cloth and let it rest for ½ hour.
3. After ½ hour, knead the dough and make orange-sized balls. Roll them into a thin 12-inch discs.
4. Dry roast both sides on a hot griddle till done.

**For the pizza sauce**

1. Heat oil in a pan. Saute garlic till light brown.
2. Deglaze the pan with wine.
3. Add tomatoes, salt and basil and simmer the sauce for 15 minutes in a covered pan. Check seasoning and keep aside.

**For the topping**

1. Blanch corn kernels in salted boiling water and reserve.
2. Simmer wine in a pan on low flame till it turns thick.
3. Pan fry the figs lightly in this sauce.

**For assembling**

1. Heat a griddle on medium flame. Apply some oil on one side of the naan pizza base and roast till it turns crisp.
2. Lower the flame and smear a ladle full of the pizza sauce on one side.
3. Place some fig slices and corn kernels on this base and sprinkle feta cheese. Cook on the griddle till the bottom of the bread becomes crisp.
4. Serve straight off the griddle, garnished with sprigs of coriander.

**Quick tip: Grate the tomatoes while making sauces, instead of chopping them. The tomato's skin gets removed while grating automatically. This will save your time of blanching and de-skinning.**

Serves: 4
Time required: 1 hour
Ease of preparation: Medium
Flavour profile: NA

# Pepper Roasted Vegetables

*This nutritious pot roast is the perfect meal to balance the after-effects of some heavy culinary indulgence. The intensity of the Shiraz Reserve's flavour and the fieriness of the white pepper make it a cracker of a dish to boot.*

## Ingredients

3 tbsp olive oil
2-3 sprigs rosemary
100 gm carrots, diced
100 gm sweet potatoes, diced
100 gm cauliflower florets
100 gm sweet corn kernels
200 ml Shiraz Reserve
100 gm broccoli, cut into florets
200 gm button mushrooms, quartered
150 gm assorted bell peppers, cut into 1-inch strips lengthwise
100 gm zucchini, cut into roundels
Salt, to taste
1 tsp white pepper, freshly crushed

## Method

1. Heat olive oil in a cast iron crock-pot.
2. Bruise the rosemary a little and stir in the oil.
3. Add sweet potato, carrots, cauliflower, sweet corn kernels and allow these to char a little.
4. Stir in the wine and allow these to cook till 3/4th done.
5. Add the remaining vegetables, salt and white pepper.
6. Stir the vegetables on high flame till they are well charred, but not burnt.
7. Serve hot.

**Quick tip: Whenever using pepper as a spice, broil it in a hot pan on low flame for 2-3 minutes to release its natural oils. Cool and pound in a mortar for maximum flavour.**

Pairing: Shiraz Reserve for its crisp, light and fruity aromas and floral undertones.

Serves: 4
Time required: 1 hour
Ease of preparation: Easy
Flavour profile:

# Masala Chai Roast Chicken

*A marinade of Cabernet Sauvignon Reserve and a homemade rub of Masala Chai makes this dish the centre of attention on your dinner table.*

## Ingredients

### For the chicken

1 whole (approximately 800 gm), cleaned

200 ml Cabernet Sauvignon Reserve

100 ml refined oil

Salt, to taste

4 tbsp Masala Chai mix

250 gm unpeeled potatoes, cut into halves

### For basting

A fistful of coriander leaves, washed and chopped

100 ml refined oil

Serves: 4
Time required: 2 hours
Ease of preparation: Easy
Ease of preparation: Medium
Flavour profile: 

Pairing: The subtle notes of light spices and blackberry in Cabernet Sauvignon Reserve accentuate the taste of barbeque meat.

## Method

1. Heat oil in a pan. Sear the coriander leaves in it till it releases an aroma.
2. Cool and blend in a food processor. Keep aside.
3. Rub chicken with some salt.
4. In a bowl, whisk wine, oil, salt and Masala Chai mix to make a smooth marinade. Marinate the chicken and potatoes for at least ½ hour.
5. After ½ hour, stuff the marinated potatoes in the chicken's cavity. Tie the chicken legs with a thread to retain the stuffing.
6. Preheat the oven to 200°C. Bake the chicken in preheated oven for 20 minutes.
7. Baste the chicken with some coriander oil to retain its moisture. Bake again for 25 minutes.
8. Let the chicken rest for 5 minutes. Remove the thread and discard.
9. Remove the roast potatoes carefully and cut the chicken into desired pieces.
10. Drizzle some coriander oil over potatoes and serve with the chicken.

**Quick tip: To make Masala Chai mix, broil 50 gm black peppercorns, 25 gm cinnamon, 10 gm cloves, 5 gm green cardamom and 10 gm dried ginger in a heavy bottomed pan. Cool and grind to a fine powder.**

# Prawn Moilee

*The simple and rustic Prawn Moilee packs an irresistible dose of flavour courtesy the coconut milk, turmeric and prawns. This mild gravy is best enjoyed with a bowlful of steamed rice.*

## Ingredients

8-10 large prawns, shelled, deveined and cleaned
1 tsp turmeric
Salt, to taste
50 ml refined oil
1 tsp mustard seeds
5-6 curry leaves
2-3 green chillies, slit
1 medium sized onion, sliced
1 medium sized tomato, sliced
100 ml Viognier
2 cups thin coconut milk
2 cups thick coconut milk
A fistful for coriander, for garnishing

## Method

1. Rinse the prawns and apply ½ tsp turmeric and some salt on it.
2. Heat oil in a pan. Add mustard seeds and allow it to splutter.
3. Stir in curry leaves, chillies, onions and tomatoes. Sauté till the onions are translucent.
4. Add the remaining turmeric powder and quickly stir fry the prawns.
5. Add in the wine and thin coconut milk. Allow the prawns to poach.
6. Check if the prawn is done and if any seasoning is needed.
7. Once prawns are cooked, stir in the thick coconut milk on high flame.
8. Wait for one quick boil and take off heat. Serve warm.

**Quick tip:** To extract coconut milk, soak fresh whole grated coconut in a cupful of warm water. Blend in a grinder till smooth. Strain the thick milk through muslin. The process can be repeated for one more time to attain thinner milk before proceeding with the recipe.

Pairing: A chilled Viognier with an elegant floral nose adds the right amount of crispness to this flavourful seafood delicacy.

Serves: 4
Time required: 1 hour
Ease of preparation: Easy
Flavour profile:

# Festive Mutton Biryani

*It is hard to think of anything better than a saffron scented mutton dum biryani to herald any momentous occasion. Add a festive glitter of colours, flavours and magic from the heart of India and watch the meal become something to cherish forever.*

## Ingredients

### For the meat

500 gm mutton with meat on the bone, cleaned
100 ml Cabernet Sauvignon
Salt, to taste
50 gm yoghurt
50 gm onions, fried
Handful of mint leaves
½ tsp turmeric
½ tsp all-spice powder
100 ml oil
150 ml water

### For the rice

2 litres water
1 tsp oil
Salt, to taste
250 gm long grain rice, washed
50 ml milk
Few saffron strands

### For assembling

50 gm pistachios, peeled
45 gm apricots
45 gm fresh pomegranate seeds
Salt, to taste

Pairing: This dish goes best with a Viognier, as its peach and lychee-like floral notes add to the biryani's sweet undertones.

## Method

### For the meat

1. In a bowl, mix wine, salt, yoghurt, fried onions, mint leaves, turmeric and all-spice powder. Add mutton pieces and toss. Let it rest in this marinade for at least ½ hour.
2. Heat oil in a pan. Sear the marinated meat on high flame.
3. Once browned, add water and stir well. Cook meat in covered pan for 30 minutes on low flame. Check meat for doneness and keep aside.

### For the rice

1. In a pan, heat water. Once it starts boiling, add the oil and salt.
2. Add the washed rice and cook till 3/4th done. Strain and keep aside.
3. Heat milk in a pan and mix saffron in it. Keep aside.

### For assembling

1. Transfer the meat in a deep thick-bottomed pan. Top with the rice.
2. Sprinkle peeled pistachios and saffron milk.
3. Cover with a lid and cook covered for 15 minutes on a low flame.
4. Garnish with pomegranate seeds and mint leaves. Serve hot.

**Quick tip: For crispy fried onions, cut onions into thin slices and rub with salt. Keep aside for 10 minutes. Squeeze the water out, then fry in hot oil till golden brown.**

Serves: 4
Time required: 2 hours
Ease of preparation: Medium
Flavour profile: 

# Pan Seared Mackerel

*This spicy fish preparation deglazed with a crisp white wine is a delicious heirloom recipe making it ideal for festive occasions.*

## Ingredients

4 fresh mackerels, cleaned and gutted

Salt, to taste

3 tbsp red chilly powder

1 tsp turmeric powder

1 tbsp coriander powder

Juice of 1 lemon

100 ml refined oil

100 ml Sauvignon Blanc

## Method

1. Make incisions on the mackerel for the spices to penetrate its meat.
2. Mix salt, chilly powder, turmeric powder and coriander powder together with lemon juice. Rub it over the fish and keep aside for 15 minutes.
3. In a frying pan, heat oil. Pan sear the fish on both sides on medium flame.
4. Once done, splash the white wine and swirl the fish. Turn once for both sides of the fish to absorb the flavour of the wine.
5. Leave it a little moist to retain some gravy.
6. Serve hot with steamed rice.

**Quick tip: To make a quick salsa, toss 100 gm diced red peppers with 5-6 chopped mint leaves, juice of half lemon and some salt in a bowl.**

Pairing: Sauvignon Blanc with its crisp lemon and passionfruit like aromas adds to the subtlety of the fresh mackerel.

Serves: 4
Time required: 30 minutes
Ease of preparation: Easy
Flavour profile:

# Chicken Lavender Pilaf

*This pilaf is a stellar combination of chicken, rice and wine, embellished with fragrance of fresh lavender flowers.*

## Ingredients

**For the meat**

100 ml Cabernet Sauvignon
Salt, to taste
50 gm yoghurt
1 tsp turmeric
2 tsp ginger-garlic paste
2 tsp chilly powder
¼ tsp Kasuri Methi, broiled and crushed
50 ml oil
500 gm chicken breast, cleaned and cubed

**For the rice**

1 tsp oil
2-3 green cardamoms
2 tbsp cashewnuts
1 tbsp golden raisins
2 litres water
Salt, to taste
250 gm long grain rice, washed

**For assembling**

2 tbsp lavender flowers

## Method

**For the meat**

1. In a bowl, mix wine, salt, yoghurt, turmeric, ginger-garlic paste, Kasuri methi and chilly powder. Marinate chicken pieces in it for at least ½ hour.
2. Preheat oven to 200°C.
3. Skewer marinated meat and bake in preheated oven for 20 minutes.
4. Rest for 10 minutes and keep aside.

**For the rice**

1. In a pan, heat oil. Add in cardamom pods, cashewnuts and raisins. Carefully add water. Once it starts boiling, add the salt.
2. Add rice and cook till 3/4th done. Strain and keep aside.

**For assembling**

1. Toss the rice and chicken in a pan.
2. Cover with a lid and cook covered for 15 minutes on a low flame.
3. Garnish with fresh lavender flowers.

**Quick tip: Want to grill chicken in a non-stick pan? Simply drizzle enough oil on the pan and sear the meat on low flame till well browned on all sides.**

Pairing: Viognier with its peach and lychee-like floral notes is an ideal accompaniment to this dish.

Serves: 4
Time required: 1.5 hours
Ease of preparation: Medium
Flavour profile:

# Squid Tempura

*This wine batter fried squid rings, topped with tangy raw mangoes, mint leaves and tomatoes make for a delightful starter.*

## Ingredients

500 gm squids, cleaned and cut into rings
4 tbsp refined oil

**For the batter**

1/8 tsp baking soda
1 tsp salt
50 gm cornstarch
150 gm rice flour
1 egg yolk
200 ml Chenin Blanc, chilled

**For assembling**

1 raw mango, sliced
1 tomato, sliced
Handful mint leaves
1 tsp chilly powder
Juice of ½ lemon

## Method

1. In a bowl, sift baking soda, salt, cornstarch and rice flour.
2. In another bowl, mix egg yolk and wine. Mix this with the dry ingredients, but avoid over-mixing.
3. Heat oil in a heavy bottomed frying pan.
4. Dip squid rings in the batter. Using a spoon, pick each ring and fry in the hot oil on high flame till golden brown.
5. Keep aside on a paper towel to drain excess oil.
6. Transfer squid rings on a serving plate. Top with mango, tomato and mint leaves. Sprinkle chilly powder and fresh lemon juice. Serve hot.

**Quick tip: Chill all the ingredients for the tempura before use. This will make the dish crispier.**

Pairing: The subtlety of Chenin Blanc with its fruity notes works wonders for this dish.

Serves: 4
Time required: 45 minutes
Ease of preparation: Medium
Flavour profile:

# Grilled Greens With Poached Eggs

*If you are hosting a party at short notice, this dish will save the day, especially when served with a beautiful collection of grilled greens on a platter.*

## Ingredients

500 ml water
1 tbsp white vinegar
4 eggs
1 tbsp refined oil
20 asparagus stalks
20 Haricot beans, stringed and halved
5-6 yellow cherry tomatoes, quartered
5-6 red cherry tomatoes, quartered
Salt, to taste
Black pepper, to taste
4 tbsp mustard mayonnaise
Handful of mustard leaves

## Method

1. Boil water in a pan. Add vinegar and reduce the flame.
2. Break eggs gently in this water and allow them to poach for 5 minutes.
3. Remove each egg with a slotted spoon and transfer to another bowl of cold water.
4. Drizzle some oil on a pan and grill asparagus and beans till done.
5. On each serving plate, transfer some grilled greens, tomatoes and one poached egg.
6. Sprinkle salt, black pepper, mustard mayonnaise and mustard greens.
7. Serve warm.

**Quick tip: Do not have the time to poach eggs? Substitute with a fried sunny-side egg instead.**

Pairing: The crisp aroma of lemon and passionfruit in a Sauvignon Blanc offers a delightful contrast to the creaminess of eggs.

Serves: 4
Time required: 30 minutes
Ease of preparation: Medium
Flavour profile: 

# Scrambled Eggs On Toast

*When family gatherings continue well into the morning hours, here's a wholesome breakfast you can whip up in a jiffy.*

## Ingredients

500 ml Chenin Blanc

1 tbsp peppercorns, crushed

100 gm salted butter, at room temperature

8 whole eggs

4 multigrain bread slices

3 onions, sliced and grilled

3 Baked potatoes, cut into wedges

2 tomatoes, halved and grilled

1 tsp flat parsley leaves, roughly chopped

## Method

1. Place a pan on medium flame and add the wine and black peppercorns. Reduce the wine till you get around 4 tablespoons. Remove from heat, cool and then chill in a refrigerator.
2. Mix the chilled reduction with softened butter and reserve till further use.
3. In a clean glass bowl, whisk in eggs and keep aside.
4. Heat 1 tablespoon of chilled wine butter on a frying pan. Ladle in the beaten egg and fold with a spatula till just done.
5. On a serving plate, place a multigrain toast and spoon out scrambled eggs over it. Place some baked potato wedges, grilled tomatoes and onions along side. Sprinkle some chopped parsley and serve hot.

**Quick tip: For extra soft scrambled eggs, add a tablespoon of whole milk while whisking the egg.**

Pairing: You can serve this dish with the same varietal you cooked it in. However, Chenin Blanc's subtle fruity notes complement the dish perfectly.

Serves: 4
Time required: 45 minutes
Ease of preparation: Medium
Flavour profile:

# Raspberry Lassi Ice Cream

*Reduce raspberry puree with red wine and what do you get? A delicious syrup with smooth texture, which when blended with yoghurt makes it a favourite for any kind of celebration.*

## Ingredients

300 ml Shiraz

350 gm castor sugar

100 ml raspberry puree

300 ml milk

300 ml sweetened whipping cream

300 gm fresh unsweetened curd

For garnish

100 gm pomegranate seeds

100 gm strawberries, cut into halves

Serves: 4
Time required: 24 hours
Ease of preparation: Easy
Flavour profile: NA

Pairing: A perfect accompaniment would be the Shiraz for its fruity notes of cherry and strawberry and its soft velvety tannins.

## Method

1. In a heavy bottomed pan, mix the wine, sugar and raspberry puree.
2. Simmer on low heat, stirring occasionally, till it is reduced to 1/3rd of the original quantity. Keep aside.
3. Using a hand whisk or electric blender, whisk the cream in a glass bowl until it forms soft peaks.
4. Stir in yoghurt and milk and whisk until well combined.
5. Fold in the reduced raspberry mixture and combine well.
6. Pour into 1 litre ice cream tub. Cover and freeze for at least six hours or overnight.
7. Remove the ice cream from the freezer and cut into chunks. Churn it in an ice cream churner till smooth and creamy.
8. Return to the same plastic tub, cover with the lid and return to the freezer until it sets.
9. Scoop out when well set. Garnish with pomegranate seeds and strawberry halves.

**Quick tip: If you do not have an ice cream churner, cut the frozen cream into chunks and churn in a food processor with a dough making blade, till the ice crystals dissolve and the mixture gets creamy.**

# Festive Soup With Halwa

*Dessert soup is an old concept in India — take Kheer, Payesh or Payasam, for instance. This festive soup with a bouquet of spices and white wine infused carrot halwa on toast add magic to this classic dessert.*

## Ingredients

### For the soup

650 ml Cabernet Sauvignon Reserve
300 ml water
1 lemon
1-inch cinnamon stick
4-5 cloves
A few fennel seeds

### For gajar halwa

250 gm carrots, peeled and grated
40 gm castor sugar
100 ml Viognier
50 gm khoya
½ tsp green cardamom powder

### For assembling

50 gm blueberries, diced
50 gm strawberries, diced
1 red apple, diced
Few orange slices
Few rusk toasts
Some micro greens, for garnish

Pairing: The mild bursts of cherries, vanilla and spices in the Cabernet Sauvignon simply uplift the experience of slurping this soup contentedly.

## Method

### For the soup

1. Chill the fruits.
2. In a heavy bottomed pan, add the wine, water and spices. Bring to the boil.
3. Lower the heat and simmer for 20 minutes.
4. Grate the lemon peel for its zest. Squeeze the juice from the lemon.
5. Once the wine has reduced to 2/3rd of its original quantity, take it off the heat. Transfer to a glass bowl and cool in the refrigerator.

### For the gajar halwa

1. Heat ghee in a heavy bottomed pan. Stir fry the carrots on high flame till they emit a nutty aroma.
2. Add in the wine and cook on high flame till all the wine is absorbed.
3. Mix in castor sugar and khoya. Sprinkle green cardamom powder and keep aside.

### For assembling

1. In a deep dish, pour the chilled soup and stir in the diced fruits.
2. Place the gajar halwa on the rusk toast and serve along side the soup.

**Quick tip: The Gajar Halwa can be made in advance and re-warmed just before service. You can also make halwa from other vegetables like potato, bottle gourd, etc, which are available throughout the year.**

Serves: 4
Time required: 1 hour
Ease of preparation: Easy
Flavour profile: NA

# Sandalwood Granita

*A granita is always welcome, irrespective of the season. The Shiraz Rosé granita, with the unusual flavour of sandalwood powder, makes for a stunning dessert. Or serve it between courses to prepare the palate for the next dish.*

## Ingredients

600 ml fresh pomegranate juice
Juice of 2 lemons
100 gm castor sugar
½ tsp sandalwood powder
120 ml Shiraz Rosé
Fresh blueberries, to garnish

## Method

1. In a clean bowl, mix the pomegranate juice, lemon juice, castor sugar, sandalwood powder and wine. Stir till the sugar in the mixture dissolves completely.
2. Place the mix into a 1 litre ice cream tub. Put it in freezer for about 1 hour.
3. Remove it and use a fork to scrape the mixture.
4. Repeat the freezing and scraping process every hour, three times, till all the juices set in clean and flaky ice crystals.
5. Serve in a goblet, garnished with fresh blueberries.

**Quick tip: To make pomegranate juice at home, either use a vegetable juicer or press the pulpy seeds over a wire sieve for fresh and tannin free juice. If you use a grinder, the tannins from the seeds will make the juice bitter.**

Pairing: Best made, and paired with, Shiraz Rosé as it renders a refreshingly light, crisp and fruity character to the granita.

Serves: 4
Time required: 3 hours
Ease of preparation: Medium
Flavour profile: NA

nine hills

# Grape Tart With Rose Jelly

*Why stick to a simple tart for festive occasions? Make it a pièce de résistance with Philadelphia cream, topped with all-season grapes, Cabernet Sauvignon jelly and mint.*

## Ingredients

### For the shortcrust pastry

200 gm refined flour
45 gm castor sugar
3 gm salt
100 gm cold unsalted butter, cut into 1-inch cubes
100 gm rolled oats
1 readymade tart shell (6 inches diameter)

### For rose jelly

10 gm gelatin leaves
3 tbsp chilled water
50 gm castor sugar
250 ml Cabernet Sauvignon
1/4th tsp rose essence

### For the filling

200 gm Philadelphia cheese
30 gm castor sugar
45 ml pomegranate juice
100 ml Cabernet Sauvignon

### For assembling

600 gm red grapes, deseeded and cut in halves
20 gm icing sugar
Mint leaves

Serves: 4
Time required: 1.5 hour
Ease of preparation: Medium
Flavour profile: NA

Pairing: Cabernet Sauvignon with its soft tannins, vanilla and berry-like aroma goes well with this dessert.

## Method

### For rose jelly

1. Break gelatin leaves in 3 tbsp chilled water and keep aside for 10 minutes.
2. Once it blooms, press all water out and reserve the gelatin.
3. Heat the wine and sugar in a saucepan on medium flame.
4. When the sugar dissolves, stir in the gelatin for a few minutes.
5. Remove from heat, add rose essence and then place the mixture over an ice bath. Keep stirring till the mixture chills and the gelatin mixes perfectly.
6. Pour this into a setting tray and place in the refrigerator till set. Cut into 1-inch cubes and reserve in the refrigerator till needed.

### For filling

1. Heat a pan. Add red wine and pomegranate juice and keep stirring till it becomes a sticky syrup.
2. Whisk Philadelphia cheese with castor sugar and pomegranate-wine syrup till it gets a creamy texture.

### For assembling

1. Spoon and spread the filling evenly in the tart shell.
2. Top with grapes, rosé jelly and mint leaves.
3. Dust icing sugar just before serving.

**Quick tip: While making tarts, chill all ingredients for better short crust.**

# Spiced Christmas Cake

*In olden days, people mixed the previous year's macerated fruits to the current year's batter for Xmas cake. Any leftover fruits would be refrigerated for the next year. Wouldn't you like to take this lovely tradition forward too?*

## Ingredients

375 gm mixed candied fruits (black currants, raisins, prunes, apricots, lemon peel, orange peel and glazed cherries)
6 tbsp brandy
125 ml Cabernet Sauvignon
125 gm refined flour
115 gm butter
115 gm soft brown sugar
4 medium-sized eggs
1 tsp cinnamon powder
1 tsp clove powder

**Quick tip: Dust fruits with flour before folding it in the batter, else it will settle to the bottom of the pan while baking.**

Serves: 6
Time required: 6 hours
Ease of preparation: Medium
Flavour profile: NA

Pairing: Make and serve at room temperature with a glass of chilled Cabernet Sauvignon. Its notes of blackberries, vanilla and light spices are apt for the flavourful, spiced cake.

## Method

1. Soak dried fruits in brandy and red wine in a clean sterilized glass bowl for a minimum of three days in the refrigerator. It is ideal if you can soak it for over a few months and keep it covered and refrigerated, if you have time at hand.
2. Preheat oven to 160°C.
3. Grease and line a 6-inch cake tin.
4. Sieve the flour and keep aside.
5. In another bowl, beat butter and sugar until soft. Gradually beat in the eggs, cinnamon powder and clove powder.
6. Mix half the flour in the fruits to lightly coat them with flour.
7. Fold the butter-egg mix and fruit-flour mixture with the remaining flour to form a smooth batter.
8. Pour the mixture into the cake tin and tap the tin gently to ensure the cake is levelled out.
9. Bake in preheated oven for 1 hour. Now reduce the temperature to 140°C and bake for 2 hours.
10. Check whether cake is done, by inserting a thin knife into the top of the cake. It should come out nice and clean. If the knife is sticky, bake the cake for another 10 to 15 minutes.
11. Switch the oven off and leave the cake in its tin, in the oven, for 30 minutes. Demould and cool on a wire rack. Cut into squares and enjoy at room temperature. You can garnish it with whipped cream, fondant and/or sliced fruits.

# Mince Pies

*The flakiness of shortcrust pastries and the richness of the Cabernet Sauvignon macerated fruits — this is the ideal treat for any celebration.*

## Ingredients

### For the filling

280 gm mixed candied fruits (black currants, raisins, prunes, apricots, lemon peel, orange peel and glazed cherries)

100 ml Cabernet Sauvignon

### For the tarts

225 gm cold butter, diced

350 gm refined flour, sieved

100 gm castor sugar

Pinch of salt

1 small egg, beaten

### For garnish

Icing sugar

Serves: 4
Time required: 4 hours
Ease of preparation: Easy
Flavour profile: NA

Pairing: Cabernet Sauvignon with its vanilla cherry and capsicum like aromas add to the intensity of these fruity tarts.

## Method

### For the filling

1. Mix candied fruits and red wine in a glass bowl.
2. Refrigerate for at least 3 days, though soaking for few months is ideal.

### For the tarts

1. Using your fingertips, mix the butter with flour, castor sugar and salt till it resembles breadcrumbs.
2. Add the beaten egg and lightly knead till the dough holds shape. Wrap in clingfilm and refrigerate for 30 minutes.
3. Preheat oven to 180°C.
4. Remove the chilled dough and roll out four discs, each ½ inch thick. Reserve some dough.
5. Press the dough discs into tart moulds and line it gently. Poke it with a fork so the tarts don't puff up in the oven.
6. Bake in preheated oven for 10 minutes and keep aside.
7. Using a cookie cutter, cut out small star shapes from the remaining dough and refrigerate it.
8. Preheat oven to 180°C again.
9. Spoon the fruit mixture into the tarts and place the chilled star shapes over it.
10. Bake in the preheated oven for 12 minutes until the stars turn golden. Let it rest for 5 minutes.
11. Remove from oven and demould carefully. Let it cool on a wire rack.
12. Before serving, dust lightly with icing sugar.

**Quick tip: To make eggless mince tarts, substitute the egg in the recipe with 1 tbsp of chilled milk.**

# Wine Glossary

| | |
|---|---|
| Acidity | Acids are present naturally in the wine or can develop during vinification. This characteristic crispy and balanced taste is called acidity. |
| Aging | It is the process of keeping wine in barrels and other containers to help the flavours develop and mature. |
| Aroma | The wine's definitive fragrance, especially in newly-bottled wine. |
| Bouquet | This defines the mix of various aromas, especially in vintage wines. |
| Dry | Caused by tannins in the wine, it is a characteristic in wine that causes puckering sensations in the mouth. |
| Fermentation | A process in vinification where yeast is used to convert grape sugars to alcohol. |
| Finish | The lingering textures and flavours in the mouth after swallowing wine. |
| Flavors | The various tastes perceived by the taste buds. |
| Fruity | The aroma and flavours of fruit in the wine. |
| Full-bodied | Wine that is high on flavours and textures. |
| Spicy | Wines that have flavours of certain spices in them. |
| Sweet | Wines that have higher sugar content in them lending it a sweet taste. |
| Tannins | These are phenolic compounds in wines that leave a slightly bitter and dry sensation in the mouth. |
| Texture | A description of how the wine tastes on the palate. |
| Vinification | The process of making wine. |
| Vintage | The year or season when the wine was bottled. |
| Wine | A beverage that is the final product of fermented grapes. |
| Yeast | A microorganism used to convert grape sugars into alcohol. |
| Yield | The productivity of a vineyard. |

LEGEND

- Dishes containing eggs, meats or seafood.
- Vegetarian dishes.

FLAVOUR PROFILE

Moderately spicy -

Spicy -

Sweet - NA